21st
Century
Skills Library

GLOBAL PERSPECTIVES

POVERTY

Robert Green

Cherry Lake Publishing
Ann Arbor, Michigan

Published in the United States of America by Cherry Lake Publishing
Ann Arbor, Michigan
www.cherrylakepublishing.com

Content Adviser: Zoë Chafe, Research Associate, Worldwatch Institute, Washington, DC

Photo Credits: Cover and page 1, © iStockphoto.com/jwebb; page 4, © Mike Goldwater/
Alamy; page 6, © E & S Ginsberg/Alamy; page 8, © David R. Frazier Photolibrary, Inc./
Alamy; pages 10 and 17, © Picture Contact/Alamy; page 12, © Kevin Foy/Alamy; page
13, © Lou Linwei/Alamy; page 15, © INTERFOTO Pressebildagentur/Alamy; page 18, ©
JUPITERIMAGES/Brand X/Alamy; pages 21 and 22, © Jim West/Alamy; page 25, © Tina
Manley/Medical/Alamy; page 26, © Richard Levine/Alamy

Map by XNR Productions Inc.

Library of Congress Cataloging-in-Publication Data
Green, Robert, 1969–
 Poverty / by Robert Green.
   p. cm.—(Global perspectives)
 Includes index.
 ISBN-13: 978-1-60279-126-8
 ISBN-10: 1-60279-126-0
 1. Poverty—Juvenile literature. 2. Poverty—United States—Juvenile
literature. I. Title. II. Series.
 HC110.P6G744 2008
 362.5—dc22   2007038838

Cherry Lake Publishing would like to acknowledge the work of
The Partnership for 21st Century Skills.
Please visit www.21stcenturyskills.org *for more information.*

TABLE OF CONTENTS

CHAPTER ONE

GOING WITHOUT

A relief worker hands out food supplies to a poor woman in Kenya.

Asger Knudsen, a sandy-haired boy from the northern European country of Denmark, stood in front of a soft-drink vending machine in a conference center, searching his pockets for change. He had just flown across the Atlantic Ocean, from his home to the city of Montreal, Canada, and he was very thirsty.

"I can't believe I don't have enough money for a soda," he said to a girl who wandered over to watch Asger. "It's only a dollar."

The girl, whose name was Marie Pepin, was very serious. "Can you imagine," she asked, "if you had only one dollar every day to live on? You certainly wouldn't be buying soft drinks from a vending machine."

"Please," said Asger, "I'm already feeling very poor at the moment, and I just want to get an orange soda. And really, how would anyone live on one dollar a day?"

"Well, mostly they would go without some of the many things that we take for granted. Anyway, that's what we are here to find out," said Marie, introducing herself to Asger.

Marie was from Montreal, and she was greeting students from all over the world who were arriving for the Global Issues **Summit**. Her conversation with Asger was her first opportunity to start talking about their topic for the conference—**poverty**. The students gathering for the conference would attempt to increase their understanding of the causes of poverty and what could be done to end it.

❋ ❋ ❋

Defined simply, poverty is when people do not have enough of the things they need to survive. This means that they cannot buy or grow enough food. But food is just the starting point. After finding food for the

A homeless person sits on a bench in New York City. There are people living in poverty in every nation in the world.

day, people must figure out how they are going to pay for their homes and buy clothing, shoes, medicine, and other necessary items. People who do not have these basic things are said to be living in poverty.

The dollar-a-day standard for measuring poverty is used by the World Bank, an international organization that studies ways to reduce poverty. The dollar is used as the measure because it's one of the world's most common currencies.

Poverty depends on many factors. In some places, food is more expensive and harder to bring to market, so even people with jobs might still live in extreme poverty.

The most telling sign of poverty is hunger, when people simply do not have enough to eat. Many poor people spend most of their time trying to obtain food and clean water.

✳ ✳ ✳

"For the poor, life is nothing but a daily struggle to live," said Marie. "It is heartbreaking to see."

As Asger was sipping his orange soda (Marie had given him a dollar), he began to feel a little uneasy. "But why," he asked, "are so many people so poor? There is plenty of food all over the world. No one should go hungry or live such a bleak life."

"That's the hard part," said Marie. "We need to figure out what causes poverty and why so many are hungry, and put a stop to it."

21st Century Content

In the early 21st century, there are half as many poor people in the world as in recent decades. This number refers to absolute poverty, or poverty that is based on living on a certain amount of money, such as one dollar, a day.

There is another way to measure how poor some people are in relation to how rich others are. This is known as income inequality. It measures the difference in the amount of money people make. It shows that a few people in the world are very rich, and many more people are poor. Wealth is unevenly distributed. While global poverty is dropping, the difference between the rich and poor is growing.

CHAPTER TWO

A Global Snapshot

A poor family stands in front of their home in Mumbai, India.

Asger finished his soda and, feeling a little glum, joined the other students at the global summit. "Poverty is kind of depressing," he said.

"It sure is," said Idrissa Diouf, a student from the West African nation of Senegal. "But there is some good news in recent poverty **trends**. There are many fewer poor people today than there were in the past."

Idrissa, an intelligent boy who liked charts and diagrams, gave a presentation on global poverty to the other students. He was particularly interested in the trends, or recent changes, in poverty numbers. His charts showed some positive developments.

✳ ✳ ✳

According to the World Bank, the number of people living in extreme poverty (those living on one dollar a day or less) dropped from 40 percent of the world's population in 1981 to 21 percent of the population in 2001. This means that after 20 years, there were only half as many people in poverty around the globe. This is a dramatic change in the right direction.

The greatest drop in poverty occurred in Asia, especially in China and India. These two countries have very large populations. In fact, they are the only two countries that have populations of more than 1 billion people. The total world population is about 6.6 billion people, so one-third of the world's people live in those two countries. China, for example, has 1 billion *more* people than the United States, which has a population of about 300 million.

While global poverty is dropping overall, the changes are not distributed evenly. Some parts of the world are actually getting poorer. In places such as eastern Europe, central Asia, and Africa, the number of people living in poverty increased from 1981 to 2001.

✳ ✳ ✳

Some poor people in Bulgaria try to make a living by searching for plastic bottles they can turn in for money at a recycling center.

"So you see," said Idrissa, "the overall picture is getting better. But in places such as Africa, where I come from, it is actually getting worse. This is very troubling for the people of Africa."

"Why is poverty getting worse in some places and better in others?" asked Marie.

"That is a very important question," said Idrissa. "To answer it, we must ask what happened in places such as China and India that reduced the number of people in poverty."

"I get it," said Asger. "And we must look at the things that happened in eastern Europe, central Asia, and Africa that made more people poor."

"That's right," said Idrissa. "The trends tell us what is happening. Then we must look closely at particular cases, such as the drop in poverty in China, and ask how it happened. The hope is that by understanding how poverty decreased or increased in one area, we can apply those lessons to other parts of the world."

21st Century Content

Globalization has tied the nations of the world closer together. There is now more trade among nations than ever before. There is a lively debate about globalization's effect on poverty. In China, there is no question that increased trade has helped reduce poverty, since China sells many goods that other nations buy. Not only has this brought more money into China, but it has provided more jobs as other countries buy more and more of China's products.

In Africa, however, globalization has had different results. Many African nations produce fruits and vegetables, but they have not been traded as freely as other products, which hurts these nations. In other countries, such as the United States, globalization has led to some job losses, especially in manufacturing. The debate will continue, since globalization is still an unfinished story.

CHAPTER THREE

CHINA: A STUDY IN REDUCING POVERTY

China is one of the most populated countries in the world.

"**I** find the case of China particularly interesting," said Marie. "Can you imagine lifting 500 million people out of poverty in 20 years? Why, that's more than the population of the United States, Canada, and Mexico combined!"

"And it happened so quickly," said Susan Hu, a student from China who was about to give a presentation on the reduction of poverty in China. "The most important factor to look at is the economic growth. China's economy has been booming in recent decades. As a result, more people have found jobs and people make more money."

Workers make shoes in a factory in China. The country's economy is booming.

"I don't understand," said Asger. "Why did the economy suddenly start to grow so quickly? What could possibly have such a large impact on something so big as a nation's economy?"

"Those are exactly the right questions!" said Susan. "And the simple answer is that China's **Communist** government made some big changes. In some areas of China, the government adopted **capitalism**. In capitalism, businesses and goods are owned by individuals. This creates an economy in which businesses grow. When businesses grow, more people have work. When more people are working, there is less poverty. Successful businesses in China now include clothing factories, electronics stores, and hotels and restaurants."

Throughout the world, as in China, countries that do not have strong economies tend to have many more poor people. When there is a strong economy, people have the opportunity to work and make money. This reduces poverty. When the economy is slow, there are fewer jobs and more poor people.

Another major factor affecting economic growth is government policy. Government leaders make many decisions that affect the economies of their countries. Therefore, they influence the number of their citizens who live in poverty. This connection is seen very clearly in the case of China.

In the late 1950s, the Communist Chinese government attempted to make China rich by encouraging the growth of industry. The Chinese saw that many countries, such as Japan and the United States, were rich in part because of their industries—specifically those involving the manufacture of goods, such as airplanes and automobiles. China wanted

Women strip the bark from a tree for food in China during the 1950s. China's Great Leap Forward failed and many people went hungry because of poor government planning.

to have factories, too. The Chinese plan, known as the Great Leap Forward, was to make China an **advanced industrial nation** in a short period of time.

But most people in China were still farmers. When the government required them to work in industries, it did not provide them with the

As economies develop, some people move away from rural areas to work in big cities. Often, their families do not move with them because it is expensive to live in a city. These new city dwellers no longer have their families nearby to provide help and support in times of need. This is happening right now in China, where so many people are moving from the countryside to cities. And in Africa, more people are moving from rural areas to cities than on any other continent in the world. Because the tradition of relying on family for help and support is being lost, government assistance programs are being created to make sure that people's basic needs are being met.

Do you think it's a good idea to rely on government services for help? Why or why not?

training they needed. In fact, the Great Leap Forward was disorganized and ineffective. It was a bold plan, but a giant failure. Since many farmers had stopped farming to work in industries, there was not enough food being grown, and the people began to starve. Millions of people in China died during that time, as poverty spread across the country.

In 1979, Chinese leaders adopted a new approach. They encouraged the Chinese people to make money in the same way as people in capitalist countries, such as the United States, Australia, and Great Britain. It also allowed people from other countries to invest money in China. This money made it possible to open factories. The government also permitted the sale of goods made in other countries, which it had never allowed before. This approach was extremely successful. China's economy began to grow rapidly, and poverty dropped just as quickly.

Many people live in poverty in Lagos, Nigeria, and other places in Africa.

✳ ✳ ✳

"The case of China shows that government policy has a direct impact on poverty," said Susan. "It can either make poverty worse or reduce poverty by stimulating economic development."

"And," said Idrissa, "it also illustrates one of the reasons that poverty in Africa has gotten worse—bad government policy and slow economies."

CHAPTER FOUR

LOOKING CLOSER TO HOME

A couple helps serve meals to the poor at a soup kitchen.
Poverty exists even in the richest countries of the world.

"But it is important to remember," said Idrissa, "that this is a big-picture view of global poverty. If we look closer at individual cases of poverty, we will discover that there are many factors that cause it."

"Not only that," said Marie, "but it also happens all over the world."

"Yes," Susan said, "poverty exists in every country to some degree or another. In any major city in the world, we can see people on the streets trying to survive."

Over the course of the summit, Asger had become more interested in poverty. It was now his turn to give a presentation to the group. He chose to talk about poverty in **developed nations**. He began with a few questions, which got all of them thinking.

"Why," he asked, "are there people in developed countries—countries with lots of money and lots of available food—who go hungry? And why are there people in these countries who have no homes and can't find jobs?"

❊ ❊ ❊

If we look at the entire world, poverty is concentrated in **developing nations**. But if we look closer at any particular country, we will find that no matter how rich a country is, there are poor people living there. To understand this, we must look once again at economics. In developed nations, to get the money to buy food, rent an apartment, or buy a house, people work at a job that pays a wage or a salary. In other words, they make money by working and use that money to pay for the things they need.

What happens, however, if people stop working? This might happen because they lose their jobs, as when a business closes in a town. It might also happen if they become sick or develop an addiction to alcohol or drugs. It might also happen if they have psychological problems that prevent them from holding a job. The most common reason that some people can't find work is that they are simply not qualified for certain jobs, or they lack the proper training to do them.

No matter what the reason may be, people without jobs run a high risk of being poor. They struggle to survive without a reliable source of income. Sometimes poverty affects entire towns or regions after a change in the local economy, such as a factory closing.

✳ ✳ ✳

"It's not just people who lose their jobs who struggle against poverty," said Asger.

Some jobs, such as working in a fast-food restaurant, may not pay enough to keep a family out of poverty.

"Some people work full time, but don't make enough money to pay for food and their most basic needs. We call these people the **working poor**."

"That's a very good point," said Marie. "Aside from absolute poverty, many people struggle to survive even if they are not technically considered poor."

"Let's not forget that there is a bit of good news in this story, too," said Idrissa. "Governments all over the world and many other groups are trying to end poverty and help people who are struggling to survive."

CHAPTER FIVE

A WORLDWIDE STRUGGLE

*Habitat for Humanity volunteers help build afordable housing
for poor people in many places around the world.*

"Since poverty is considered a global problem affecting all of us," said

Marie, "people everywhere are fighting to reduce poverty."

"If there is one thing that we have learned about poverty these past few days," said Asger, "it's that it exists everywhere, and there are many ways we can help."

❉ ❉ ❉

Poverty can be found all over the world. Though it is present in developed nations, it is more concentrated in developing nations. This has led to international efforts to get rid of poverty in developing nations by building up the economies of those nations. Aid efforts also provide basic needs such as food, clothing, shelter, and education.

Governments around the world assist in building countries' economies either by direct aid—donating machinery, giving technical advice on industry, or giving money—or by indirect aid. Indirect aid is often money donated to international organizations, such as the United Nations. The United Nations, which encourages international cooperation, has many programs intended to support economic development and to reduce poverty by other means.

There are also groups that help everyday people fight poverty. These groups are known as **nongovernmental organizations** (NGOs). Some of these NGOs fight the effects of drought or famine by organizing food, shelter, and medical donations. Other groups focus on long-term strategies to reduce poverty. This might include improving local farming methods to ensure more food is produced on each plot of land. It might also mean job

Life & Career Skills

Governments and nongovernmental organizations agree that poor people and poor nations need help. But they often disagree about how to help them. In this debate, a story about fish often comes up. It goes like this: Give a person a fish, and you feed that person for a day. Teach a person to fish, and they will be able to feed themselves for a lifetime.

In other words, some people argue that giving food to hungry people is far less helpful than teaching them to grow food. Or giving people some money is less likely to end poverty than helping them find a job. They believe that developing people's skills is more beneficial than giving people food or money. The difference is that one is a short-term solution, the other a long-term solution. What do you think? Should people working to reduce poverty concentrate on short-term solutions, long-term solutions, or a combination of both?

training in areas where people have lost jobs because of changes in the local economy. Or it might mean funding educational or health care programs.

Some government and NGO aid programs attempt to reduce poverty globally. At the same time, many governments try to reduce poverty within their own borders. A person who becomes unemployed, for example, can sometimes collect an unemployment check for a period of time. This money is given to the person by the government to help during hard times. Then the worker needs to find another job and support himself or herself again. Some countries also provide food for people without enough money to buy it and provide shelter for the homeless.

These government programs are paid for through **taxes**. We pay taxes when we earn money or buy certain products, so

A medical volunteer teaches poor people in Honduras about basic health and sanitation.

"government" programs are really paid for by the people of the country. And they are available to all citizens, if they fall on hard times.

✳ ✳ ✳

*Volunteers at a neighborhood food pantry fill
bags with groceries for people in need.*

"There are also some very practical things that we can do if we want to help fight poverty locally," said Idrissa. "For example, we know that the better educated people are, the less likely they are to be poor. So we can help teach people to read, or we can tutor children who have problems learning in school."

"In Denmark, we also have many places where homeless people can get food and shelter," said Asger. "People can volunteer to help work in these places, or they can help a private charity."

"And many people choose to donate money to groups that fight poverty around the world," said Marie.

"It seems quite clear," said Susan, still thinking about the dramatic drop in poverty in China, "that we need both government policies to help keep economies strong and also private citizens who are willing to help those who are struggling just to get by."

"Yes," agreed Idrissa. "If governments and citizens work together, we're sure to make progress in the fight against poverty!"

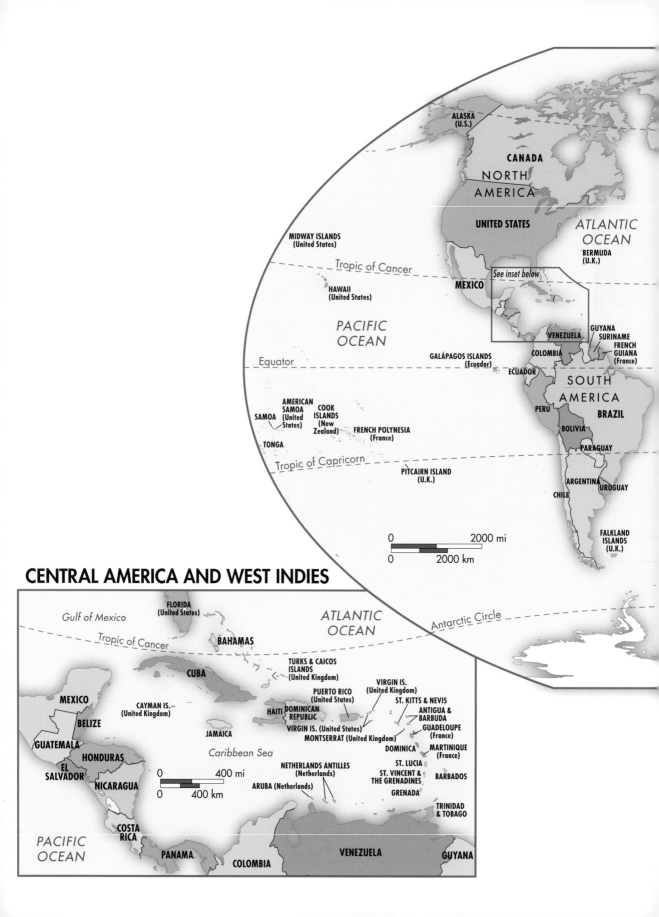

ALASKA
(U.S.)

CANADA

NORTH
AMERICA

UNITED STATES

ATLANTIC
OCEAN

BERMUDA
(U.K.)

MIDWAY ISLANDS
(United States)

Tropic of Cancer

See inset below

MEXICO

HAWAII
(United States)

GUYANA
SURINAME
FRENCH
GUIANA
(France)

VENEZUELA

COLOMBIA

PACIFIC
OCEAN

GALÁPAGOS ISLANDS
(Ecuador)

Equator

ECUADOR

SOUTH
AMERICA

PERU

BRAZIL

AMERICAN
SAMOA
(United
States)

COOK
ISLANDS
(New
Zealand)

BOLIVIA

SAMOA

FRENCH POLYNESIA
(France)

PARAGUAY

TONGA

Tropic of Capricorn

PITCAIRN ISLAND
(U.K.)

ARGENTINA

URUGUAY

CHILE

0   2000 mi

0   2000 km

FALKLAND
ISLANDS
(U.K.)

CENTRAL AMERICA AND WEST INDIES

FLORIDA
(United States)

ATLANTIC
OCEAN

Antarctic Circle

Gulf of Mexico

Tropic of Cancer

BAHAMAS

TURKS & CAICOS
ISLANDS
(United Kingdom)

VIRGIN IS.
(United Kingdom)

MEXICO

CUBA

PUERTO RICO
(United States)

ST. KITTS & NEVIS

CAYMAN IS.
(United Kingdom)

HAITI
DOMINICAN
REPUBLIC

ANTIGUA &
BARBUDA

BELIZE

GUADELOUPE
(France)

GUATEMALA

JAMAICA

VIRGIN IS. (United States)
MONTSERRAT (United Kingdom)

MARTINIQUE
(France)

HONDURAS

Caribbean Sea

DOMINICA

EL
SALVADOR

0   400 mi

NETHERLANDS ANTILLES
(Netherlands)

ST. LUCIA
ST. VINCENT &
THE GRENADINES

NICARAGUA

0   400 km

ARUBA (Netherlands)

BARBADOS

GRENADA

PACIFIC
OCEAN

COSTA
RICA

TRINIDAD
& TOBAGO

PANAMA

COLOMBIA

VENEZUELA

GUYANA

Glossary

advanced industrial nation (ad-VANST in-DUHSS-tree-uhl NAY-shuhn) a country with a high level of industrial development, such as Japan, Canada, most nations in Europe, and the United States

capitalism (CAP-uh-tul-ihzm) a way of organizing a country's economy so that all the land, houses, factories, etc., belong to private individuals rather than the government

Communist (KOM-yuh-nist) describing a way of organizing a country so that all the land, houses, factories, etc., belong to the government or community, and the profits are shared by all

developed nations (dih-VEL-uhpt NAY-shuhnz) countries with advanced levels of industrialization and generally high incomes; usually the world's richest nations, including Japan, the United States, and most nations in Europe among others

developing nations (dih-VEL-uhp-eeng NAY-shuhnz) nations in which many people are poor and industry is growing

nongovernmental organizations (NGO) (NON-GUHV-urn-mehnt-uhl or-guh-nuh-ZAY-shuhnz) organizations that are independent of governments and are not businesses; they often address problems such as development, hunger, poverty, and health issues

poverty (POV-ur-tee) a condition in which people do not have the basic things they need, such as food and shelter

summit (SUHM-it) a meeting of high-level leaders from different nations that addresses an international concern

taxes (TAKS-ehz) money collected by the government from private citizens that is then used to pay for government programs

trends (TRENDZ) a pattern or general course of events

working poor (WORK-ing POR) people who have jobs and generally work full time but cannot make enough money to pay their basic expenses, such as food and shelter

For More Information

Books

Bowden, Rob. *World Poverty*. Austin, TX: Raintree Steck-Vaughn, 2003.

Haugen, David M., and Matthew J. Box. *Poverty*. San Diego, CA: Greenhaven Press, 2006.

Senker, Cath. *Poverty*. Milwaukee, WI: World Almanac Library, 2007.

Web Sites

Kids Can Make A Difference
www.kidscanmakeadifference.org/quiz.htm
Take an online quiz to learn more about what you can do to help fight hunger and poverty

Youthink! But Do You Know?
youthink.worldbank.org
Visit this World Bank site to find out what you can do to help in the fight against poverty and hunger

INDEX

ABOUT THE AUTHOR

Robert Green has written more than 30 books for students. He is a regular contributor to publications on East Asia by the Economist Intelligence Unit and holds graduate degrees from New York University and Harvard University.